SUPER SANDCASTLE
It's the Alphabet!

It's H!

Katherine Hengel

Consulting Editor, Diane Craig, M.A./Reading Specialist

ABDO
Publishing Company

Published by ABDO Publishing Company, 8000 West 78th Street, Edina, Minnesota 55439. Copyright © 2010 by Abdo Consulting Group, Inc. International copyrights reserved in all countries. No part of this book may be reproduced in any form without written permission from the publisher. Super SandCastle™ is a trademark and logo of ABDO Publishing Company.

Printed in the United States.

♻ PRINTED ON RECYCLED PAPER

Editor: Liz Salzmann
Content Developer: Nancy Tuminelly
Cover and Interior Design and Production: Kelly Doudna, Mighty Media
Photo Credits: iStockphoto (Jani Bryson), Shutterstock

Library of Congress Cataloging-in-Publication Data
Hengel, Katherine.
  It's H! / Katherine Hengel.
      p. cm. -- (It's the Alphabet!)
  ISBN 978-1-60453-595-2
  1. English language--Alphabet--Juvenile literature. 2. Alphabet books--Juvenile literature. I. Title.
  PE1155.H466 2010
  421'.1--dc22
  ⟨E⟩
                        2009020947

Super SandCastle™ books are created by a team of professional educators, reading specialists, and content developers around five essential components—phonemic awareness, phonics, vocabulary, text comprehension, and fluency—to assist young readers as they develop reading skills and strategies and increase their general knowledge. All books are written, reviewed, and leveled for guided reading, early reading intervention, and Accelerated Reader® programs for use in shared, guided, and independent reading and writing activities to support a balanced approach to literacy instruction.

About SUPER SANDCASTLE™

Bigger Books for Emerging Readers
Grades K–4

Created for library, classroom, and at-home use, Super SandCastle™ books support and engage young readers as they develop and build literacy skills and will increase their general knowledge about the world around them. Super SandCastle™ books are an extension of SandCastle™, the leading preK–3 imprint for emerging and beginning readers. Super SandCastle™ features a larger trim size for more reading fun.

Let Us Know
Super SandCastle™ would like to hear your stories about reading this book. What was your favorite page? Was there something hard that you needed help with? Share the ups and downs of learning to read. We want to hear from you! Send us an e-mail.

sandcastle@abdopublishing.com

Contact us for a complete list of SandCastle™, Super SandCastle™, and other nonfiction and fiction titles from ABDO Publishing Company.

www.abdopublishing.com • 8000 West 78th Street
Edina, MN 55439 • 800-800-1312 • 952-831-1632 fax

Aa Bb Cc Dd Ee

Ff Gg Hh Ii Jj Kk

Ll Mm Nn Oo Pp

Qq Rr Ss Tt Uu Vv

Ww Xx Yy Zz

The Letter

Hh

H and **h** can also look like

Hh **Hh** Hh Hh Hh Hh

4

The letter **h** is a consonant.

It is the 8th letter of the alphabet.

horse

house

6

Hailey

Hailey hears a huge, happy horse behind her house.

ch as in **ch**oose

cherry

chips

chicken

8

Richard

For lunch Richard chooses chicken, cherries, and chips.

starfish

shell

Shannon shows Josh starfish and shells she found on the shore.

☞ wh as in **wh**en

whistle

whale

No words end with wh.

When whales blow whistles, pinwheels whirl everywhere.

pinwheel

th as in **think**

moth

path

Theo thinks he saw three moths on the path through the north woods.

☞ th as in **their**

clothes

Heather and her brother gather clothes and feathers together.

feather

13

Holly is happy in her house on the hill.

She likes her hammock and her neighbor Bill.

Holly has hundreds of bright fish in a tank.

"Those fish are so handsome," says her father Hank.

Holly does her homework in the kitchen one day.

Her father hints that they will soon move away.

Holly hopes in her heart
that it isn't true.

She hangs out with her fish
because she is blue.

Her hurried father honks
the horn when it is time to go.

He says, "You might like the
new house, Holly. You never know."

19

"Oh, heavens!" sighs Holly.
She sees a whale and starfish!

A house on the beach has
always been her wish.

Which words start
with the letter **h**?

fish

hammock

horse

house

cherry

pinwheel

heart

horn

23

Glossary

chip (pp. 8, 9) – a very thin slice of potato that is cooked in oil.

choose (pp. 8, 9) – to pick one of two or more options.

hammock (pp. 15, 22) – a net or cloth hung by cords at each end so that you can lie on it.

handsome (p. 16) – having a pleasing appearance.

pinwheel (pp. 11, 23) – a light wheel that is attached to a stick so it can spin in the wind.

sigh (p. 20) – to let out a loud breath that expresses a feeling such as relief, frustration, or sadness.

tank (p. 16) – a large container for fish and reptiles to live in.

whirl (p. 11) – to move quickly in circles.

whistle (p. 11) – a device that makes a shrill sound.

To promote letter recognition, letters are highlighted instead of glossary words in this series. The page numbers above indicate where the glossary words can be found.

More Words with **H**

Find the **h** in the beginning, middle, or end of each word.

chair	hard	hole	hurt	rich
eight	hat	holiday	light	school
elephant	hello	home	machine	sheep
ghost	help	hop	mother	thing
ham	hen	hot	phone	what
hand	hit	how	rhino	witch